Sea, Sky and Spaciousness

Catherine Anderson

Sea, Sky and Spaciousness

A Visual Journal
of the Eastern Shore of Virginia

Catherine Anderson

There is one spectacle grander than the sea,
That is the sky;
There is one spectacle grander than the sky,
That is the interior of the soul.

Victor Hugo

Enlightenment is when a wave
realizes it is the ocean.
Thich Nhat Hanh

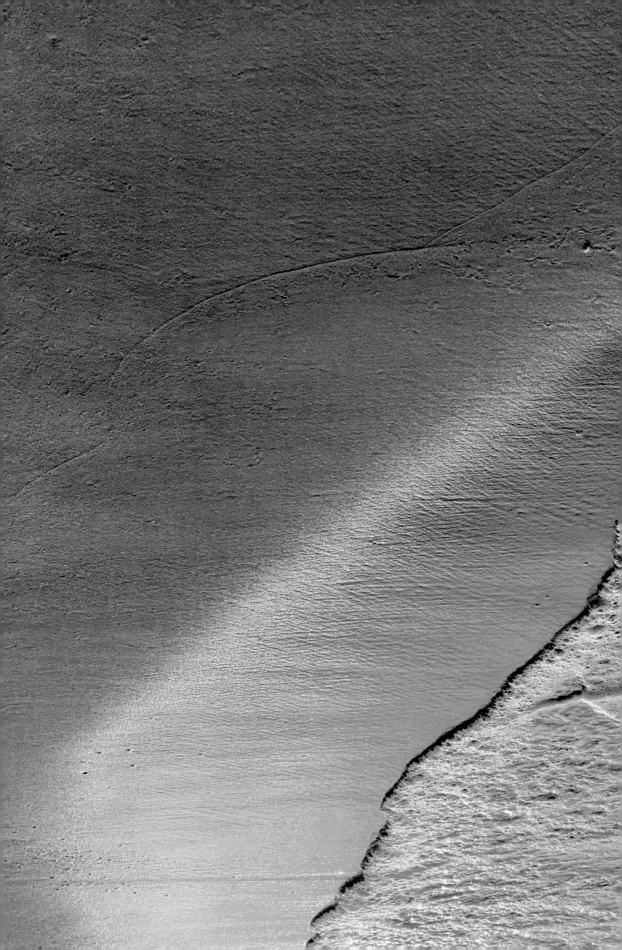

*Life is magic,
the way nature works seems to be
quite magical.*
Jonas Salk

Feelings come and go like clouds in a windy sky.
Conscious breathing is my anchor.
Thich Nhat Hanh

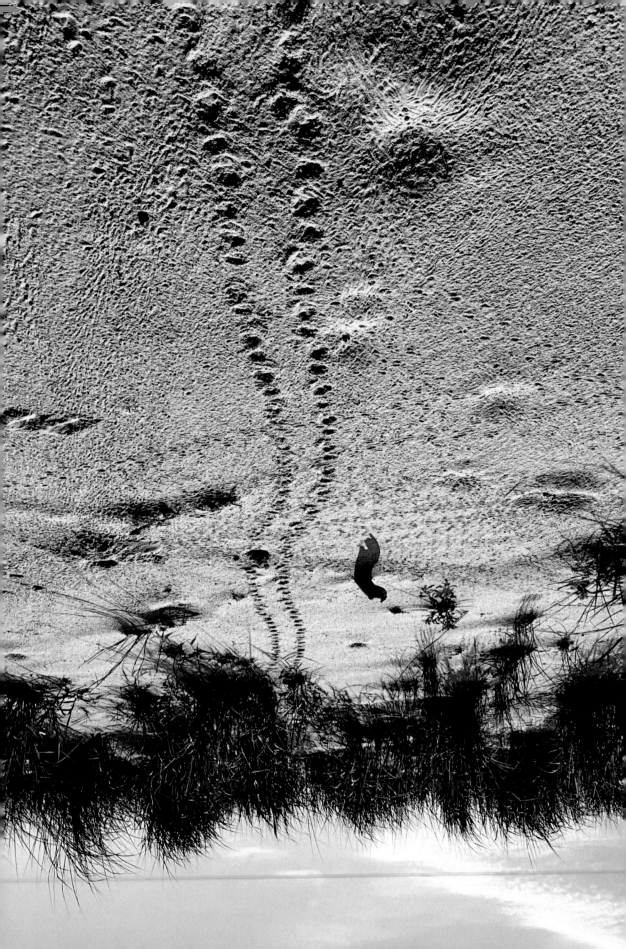

*In all things of nature there is something
of the marvelous.*
Aristotle

Wilderness is not a luxury
but a necessity of the human spirit.
Edward Abbey

The sea, once it casts its spell,
holds one in its net of wonder forever.
Edward Abbey

We have the capacity to receive messages
from the stars and the songs of the night winds.

Ruth St. Denis

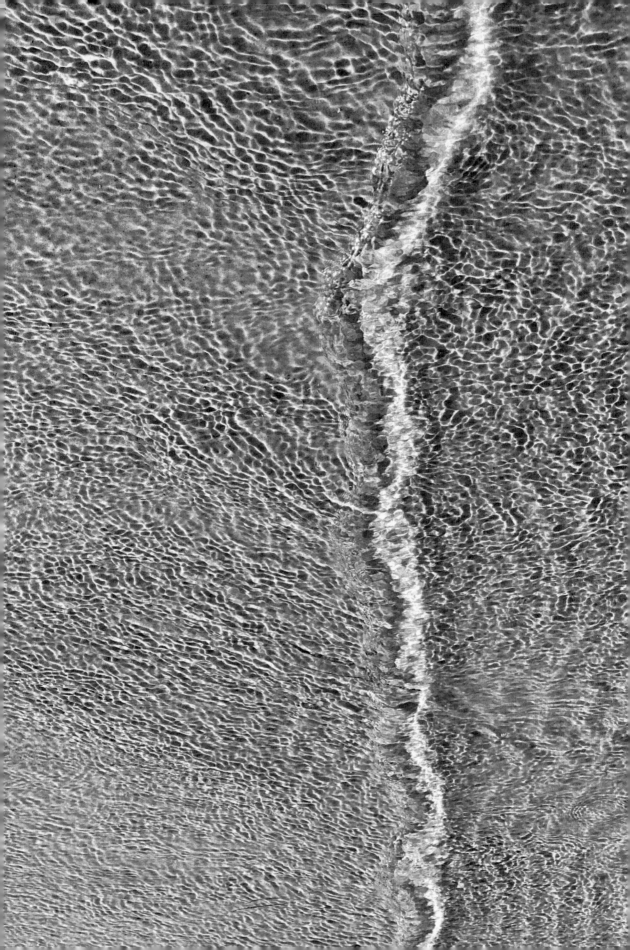

The world is always in movement.
V.S. Naipaul

I go to nature to be soothed and healed,
and to have my senses put in order.
John Burroughs

*In every walk with nature
one receives far more than he seeks.*

John Muir

My soul is full of longing for the secrets of the sea,
and the heart of the great ocean
sends a thrilling pulse through me.
Henry Wadsworth Longfellow

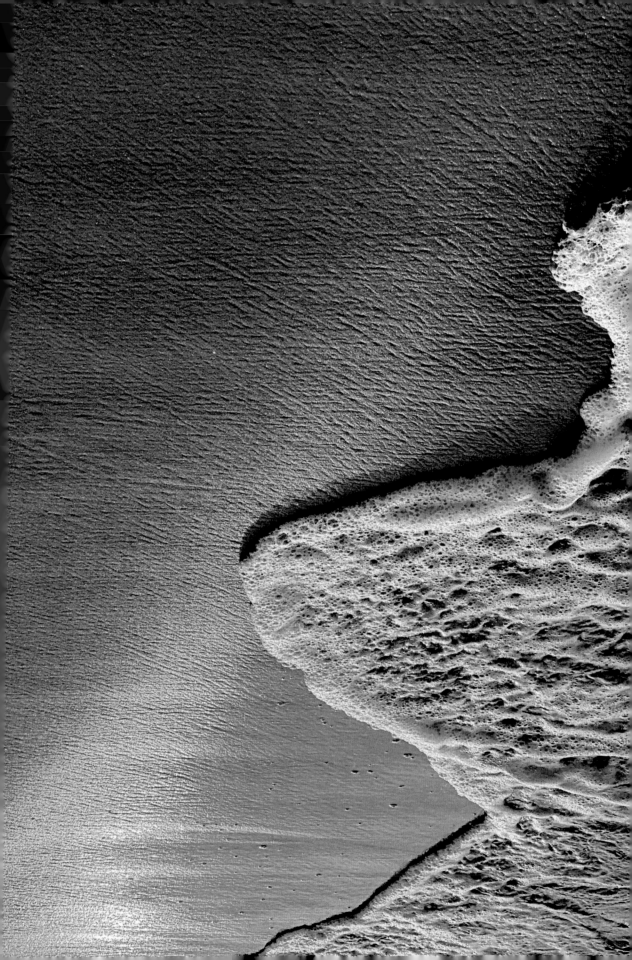

Joy is not in things; it is in us.
Charles Wagner

Behold the miracle of the earth
with all the wonder of a child.
Edna Jaques

You are the sky.
Everything else – it's just the weather.
Pema Chödrön

If there is magic on this planet,
it is contained in water.
Loren Eiseley

*And forget not that the earth delights
to feel your bare feet and the winds long
to play with your hair.*

Khalil Gibran

Those who contemplate the beauty of earth
find reserves of strength that will endure
as long as life lasts.
Rachel Carson

The mystical is not how the world is,
but that it is.
Ludwig Wittgenstein

The miracle is not to walk on water.
The miracle is to walk on the green earth in the present moment,
to appreciate the peace and beauty that are available now.
Thich Nhat Hanh

We live only to discover beauty.
All else is a form of waiting.
Kahil Gibran

Our work here is to connect with beauty,
a major source of creativity and generativity.
Beauty feeds the soul, and the soul
feeds the creative fire.

Angeles Arrien

The wisdom of nature speaks to us heart by heart.
And nature's first language is beauty.
Tim McNulty

In every man's heart there is a secret nerve
that answers to the vibrations of beauty.
Christopher Darlington Morley

If I had influence with the good fairy ...
I should ask that her gift to each child in the world
be a sense of wonder so indestructible that it would
last throughout life.
Rachel Carson

Though we travel the world over to find the beautiful
we must carry it with us or we find it not.
Ralph Waldo Emerson

Wonder is the beginning of wisdom.
Socrates

One cannot but be in awe when one contemplates
the mysteries of eternity, of life, of the marvelous
structure of reality ...
Never lose a holy curiosity.
Albert Einstein

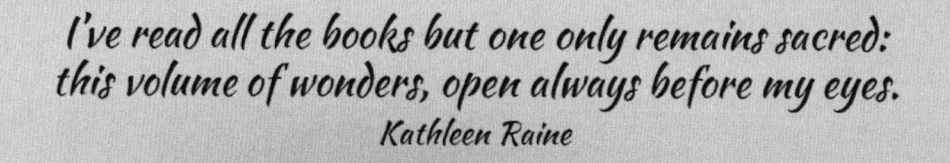

I've read all the books but one only remains sacred:
this volume of wonders, open always before my eyes.
Kathleen Raine

Learn to see, and then you'll know
that there is no end to the new worlds of our vision.

Carlos Castaneda

There is a twofold meaning in every creature,
a literal and a mystical, and the one
is but the ground of the other.

John Smith

About Catherine

Catherine Anderson is fortunate enough to spend her days creating in her studio overlooking the waters of the Chesapeake Bay and leading creative pilgrimages to beautiful places around the world.

Catherine loves introducing others to the inner processes that she considers soul languages, such as SoulCollage®, the labyrinth, contemplative photography and visual journaling. She loves watching as retreat participants open up to their own creative gifts and start sharing them in the world.

When Catherine is not playing in her studio near Cape Charles or teaching, you can find her quietly walking the beaches on the tip of the Eastern Shore of Virginia and volunteering at Kiptopeke State Park picking up trash that floats on to the beach from the Bay.

The photographs in this book were all created in and around the Chesapeake Bay area of the Eastern Shore of Virginia on one of Catherine's many beach wandering walks.

For more information visit Catherine's website
www.creativepilgrimage.com

Made in the USA
Monee, IL
23 December 2022

23492112R00040